T0132317

Kissed by Déjà vu

Anisah Hassan

To order additional copies of this book, contact:
Xlibris
844-714-8691
www.Xlibris.com
Orders@Xlibris.com

ISBN:	Softcover	978-1-4771-4381-0
	EBook	978-1-4691-2852-8

Print information available on the last page

Rev. date: 06/08/2022

Dedication

ANGELA SIMPSON
Thank you for all of the advice you served
And us sitting at the table enjoying music to sooth our nerves
Keep holding my hand and I'll hold yours
You're all a little sister could ever dream of.
Love you Annie

In the name of God, The Beneficent, The Merciful

Geraldine Simpson: My mother, one of the strongest, smartest woman I know. Don't forget to remember how much I love you.

Bridget Simpson: My twin sister, keep the laughter coming. Thanks for doing for my mom what I am unable too. Remember I'm always with you when you're right.

Nathaniel Dear: My brother from another mother (Margie Lee). I want to thank you for telling me like it is even when I don't want to hear it. You're the yin to my yang.

Aletrice (Akua) Walker: My sister with wisdom beyond. The voice of reason, vision of beauty, my zen. I know I'm a challenge, but continue to hang in there with me.

Louise (Weezy) Johnson and Gloria Green: My precious Godmothers. Thanks for caring and trying to teach me lessons to live by

Angela, Darryl, Robin, Dennis Eric Simpson: You are my mother's pride and joy. You make her happy, therefore, whats mine is yours. Love you.

Melissa, Danielle, Kandies, Kiana, Erica, Brittany, Rachelle, Shonte, Sierra, Keisha, Kelly, Gabriellyah, Terrell, Tia: You are all diamonds in the rough. Here's to use growing closer. I hope I've been a positive influence on you. Continue to grow and blossom for I am watching and learning dear ones.

Bro Sultan Muhammad: As Salaam Alaikum to you and your family, hang in there my beloved brother.

Dr. Muhammad Al-Lozi: As Salaam Alaikum to you. Thanks for the wisdom and knowledge you share and making sure I get the very best care.

Dr. Tipu Sultan: As Salaam Alaikum to you. Thanks for all the wisdom and knowledge. Continue to try to teach your sister, and providing the best of care.

Dr. Deloris Greebe- Jones: Thanks for all the knowledge and things you are teaching me every week. I'm stronger you know!

Marty, Tina, Nina: You're the best. Keep up the good work. Thanks for bearing with me and knowing my needs for Doc.

BJC Floor of Neurology: To all the nurses, techs, housekeepers for all hugs and kisses every month. Dietary you make me happy, I thank you for accommodating my diet. You all make things easier for me and I love you for that.

Mrs. Purnell: Elementary School Teacher. You encouraged me to write and made me stand before the many laughing school children to read and recite poetry for my grade. I'm better because of that!

Mrs. Scott: My Enrichment lab teacher that taught me poetry and allowing me to choose my own reports to write. Remember Mrs. Scott? My first report was Phyllis Wheatley.

Special thanks to the many Holistic and Naturalpathic MD's and Practitioners that have treated and guided me along the way.

Too all of those unnamed, but have extended kindness to me, I bestow my deepest thanks I am deeply appreciative off all my friends, family, and acquaintances, who merit special mention and have my love.

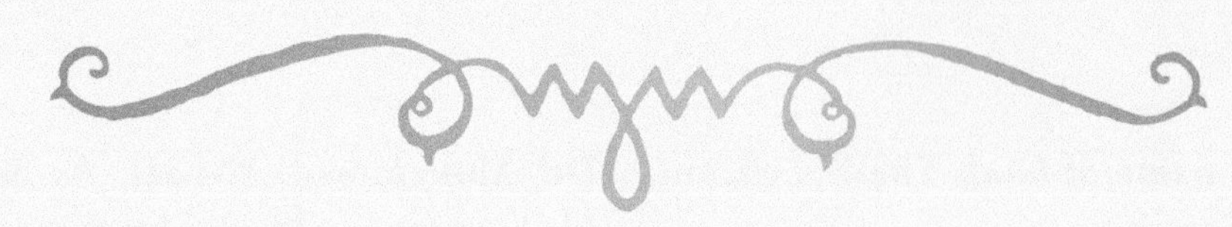

THAT'S THE BEAUTY OF LIFE

We have the sun, moon, and stars to guide us. We have oceans, mountains, the sea. That's the beauty of life.

I have some questions for you, and I really want an answer my friend. Are you immune to the trials of life? Who is your provider? Can that source guide, restore, and renew your spirit? Try to envision an infinite love without contingencies. It supersedes our declining economy and heals the morality of those with declining health, down spiraling ethics, and troubled minds.

Sure it's easy for one to utter, "don't you worry", when you are asking, Is there hope for me? Why is it taking so long? How much must I withstand, and how long can I endure? I would like to suggest that you take a moment of silence, and really take inventory of the mind. I'm quite sure that you will find, by directing your energy inward you will begin to find some of the answers you've been seeking, and longing for. Now no one said it would be easy. You've got to believe in the power of the mind and its impact on your life and your surroundings.

One cannot walk around in defeat and you must be open to change. Don't allow fear to discourage you, cast it aside. It is contagious and will overtake you and those around. Take possession of self and utilize your faith. Give it all of your energy and you will find that "Surely After Every Difficulty Comes Ease". "Joy will come with the morning".

My inner child speaking now, this may sound unrealistic, but I truly wish the world had all happy people, with no afflictions, and misery unknown. What a phenomenon it would be. I often ask myself what is life all about and my purpose in it? Am I living up to my fullest potential? I'm searching surely. I may never know the answers. Now let's be realistic here. One would have to be cold and heartless to not have concerns about self, others, and the world in which we live. Let's check the record from Prophet Adam to Muhammad (peace be upon them). I know that as I examine and explore history, I find that I am a firm believer in miracles. Time and time again we are shown the presentation from pass to present, of situations where the supernatural presents itself. That's the workings of "The Merciful". Show me your troubles and I'll show you a place where "The Most High" dwells to intervene and heal all dilemmas.

I'm not exempted.

Do I suffer and struggle with life's storms and challenges: Of course I do!.
Do I have feelings of impaired esteem, and despair? Of course I do!
Do I question the sincerity of others, and adversarial forces in my midst? Of course I do! You see, it's that divine intervention that I've been speaking of must kick in. It forces those challenges and struggles in our lives to elevate us to be more stronger and wiser. This is what makes us rearrange ourselves and the world around us. It makes us speak to our hearts, open it wide to enabling the message to transmit, encouraging us to get busy, and put in the work that it takes to yet take one more attempt at making things better in our lives and the lives of others. Just take a little time to think about what you're doing and seek guidance to understand why.

That's where the never ending cycle of life's energy occurs. It never dissipates. It simply continues recreating and rotating in another place and time, touching spirits over and over. It flows through rivers, crosses oceans, and reaches pecks of the highest mountains.

THAT'S THE BEAUTY OF LIFE.

Peace and Blessings

Anisah

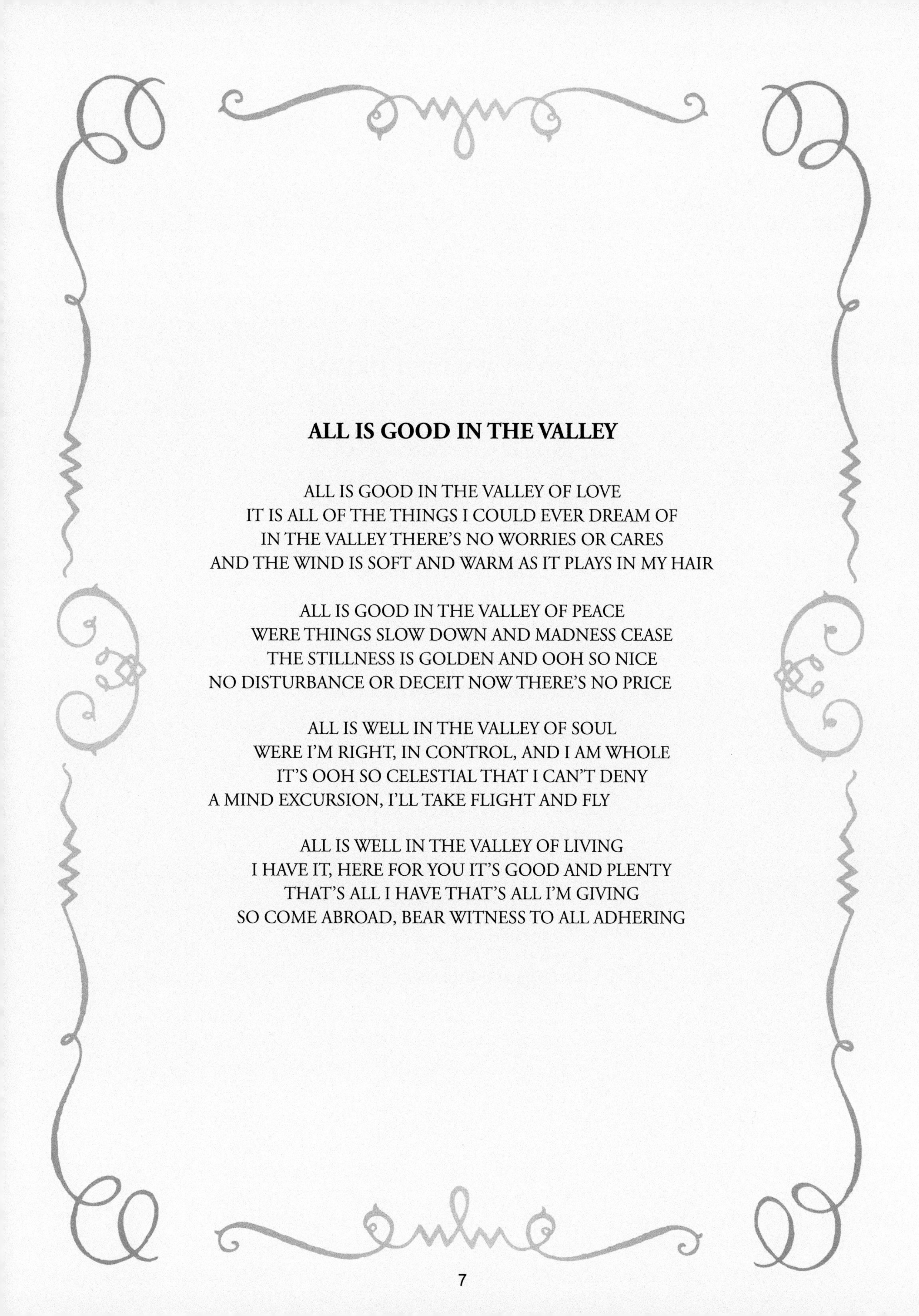

ALL IS GOOD IN THE VALLEY

ALL IS GOOD IN THE VALLEY OF LOVE
IT IS ALL OF THE THINGS I COULD EVER DREAM OF
IN THE VALLEY THERE'S NO WORRIES OR CARES
AND THE WIND IS SOFT AND WARM AS IT PLAYS IN MY HAIR

ALL IS GOOD IN THE VALLEY OF PEACE
WERE THINGS SLOW DOWN AND MADNESS CEASE
THE STILLNESS IS GOLDEN AND OOH SO NICE
NO DISTURBANCE OR DECEIT NOW THERE'S NO PRICE

ALL IS WELL IN THE VALLEY OF SOUL
WERE I'M RIGHT, IN CONTROL, AND I AM WHOLE
IT'S OOH SO CELESTIAL THAT I CAN'T DENY
A MIND EXCURSION, I'LL TAKE FLIGHT AND FLY

ALL IS WELL IN THE VALLEY OF LIVING
I HAVE IT, HERE FOR YOU IT'S GOOD AND PLENTY
THAT'S ALL I HAVE THAT'S ALL I'M GIVING
SO COME ABROAD, BEAR WITNESS TO ALL ADHERING

BEYOND MY WILDEST DREAMS

NEVER IN MY WILDEST DREAMS
IT'S REALLY SO STRANGE TO ME
THAT IN MY VERY HEART AND SOUL
I'D HAVE SUCH EXTREMES TO DEEM

I'VE HEARD OF LUST I'VE HEARD OF LIKE
BUT THIS IS NEITHER ONE
MUST GO OUTSIDE IN THE POURING RAIN
UNTIL MY PURGE IS DONE

AND WAY BEYOND MY WILDEST DREAMS
I KNOW RELISHED IN THE GLOW
YET THAT WAS LONG AGO I'VE GROWN
I'D HAVE TO LET ONE KNOW

WHO SHALL IT BE I LOVE YOU BOTH
BUT HEARTS ARE AT STAKE
AND STANDARDS TO UPHOLD
IT HURT ME SO I KNOW ONE HAS TO GO

IT IS SO EXTREME
I'LL LAY A BIT,'SLEEP ON TO MY REDEEM
THIS IS A HURT I'VE NEVER KNOWN
BEYOND MY WILDEST DREAM

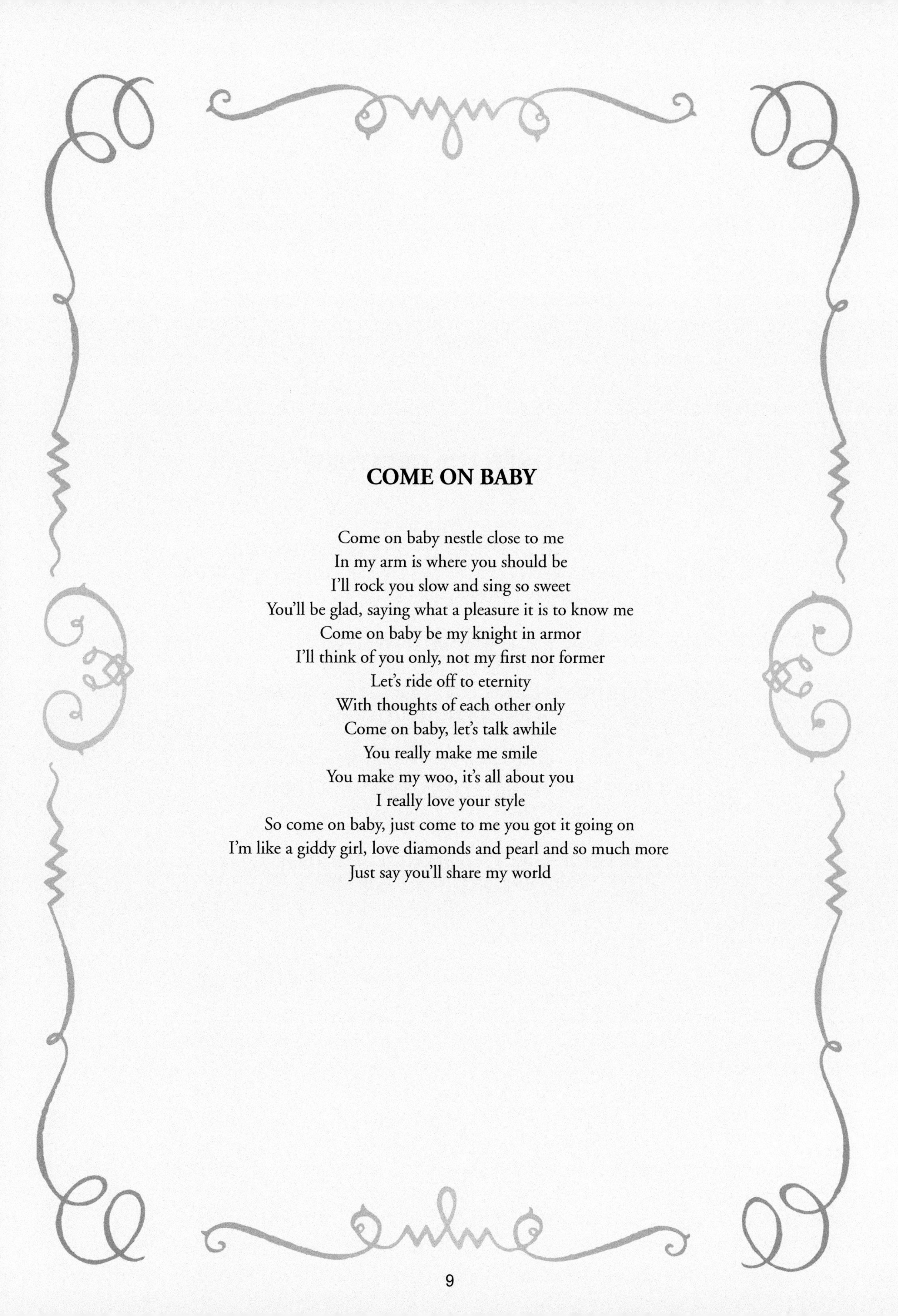

COME ON BABY

Come on baby nestle close to me
In my arm is where you should be
I'll rock you slow and sing so sweet
You'll be glad, saying what a pleasure it is to know me
Come on baby be my knight in armor
I'll think of you only, not my first nor former
Let's ride off to eternity
With thoughts of each other only
Come on baby, let's talk awhile
You really make me smile
You make my woo, it's all about you
I really love your style
So come on baby, just come to me you got it going on
I'm like a giddy girl, love diamonds and pearl and so much more
Just say you'll share my world

DESTINED FOR GREATNESS

WHEN I WAS JUST A LITTLE GIRL
I KNEW I WAS DESTINED TO DO GREAT THINGS
NOT CONCERNED WITH FANCY CARS LITTLE THINGS AND BLING
JUST DREAMING OF MY DESTINY, IT'S SURE AND MEANT FOR ME

NOW YOU KNOW WITH MY DESTINY
I LOVE IT FOR THERE'S NO STRINGS
GREATNESS FOR ME THE THOUGHTS IT BRINGS
IS JOY AND DELIGHT TO CLING

LIKE RAINBOWS IN SPRING
RIVERS, NILES THAT FLOWS, AND SUCH THINGS
JUST MAKES ME WANT TO SING

IT'S SURE, PURE FATE NO FOOLISH SCHEMES
APPOINTED AND ALL FOR ME

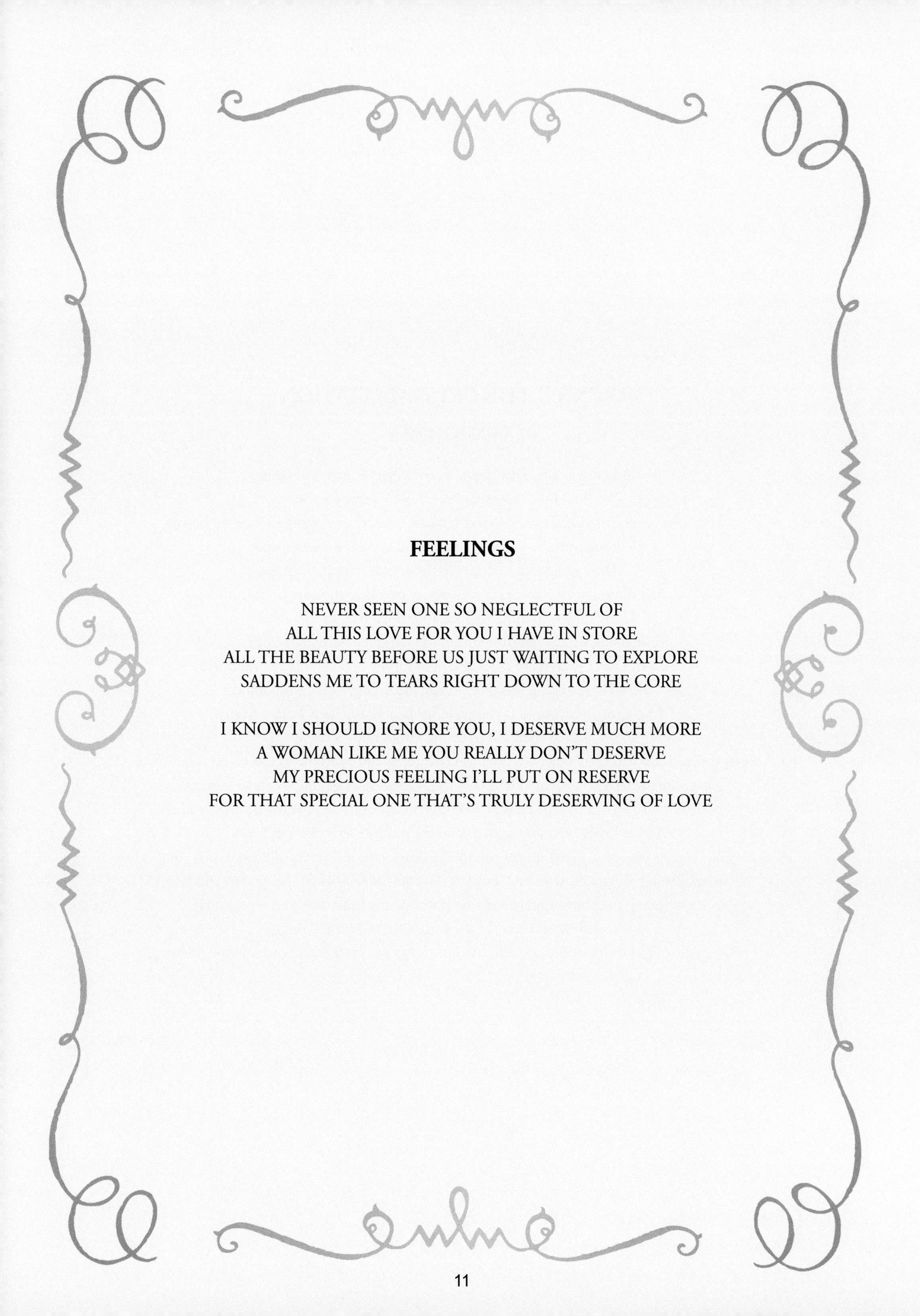

FEELINGS

NEVER SEEN ONE SO NEGLECTFUL OF
ALL THIS LOVE FOR YOU I HAVE IN STORE
ALL THE BEAUTY BEFORE US JUST WAITING TO EXPLORE
SADDENS ME TO TEARS RIGHT DOWN TO THE CORE

I KNOW I SHOULD IGNORE YOU, I DESERVE MUCH MORE
A WOMAN LIKE ME YOU REALLY DON'T DESERVE
MY PRECIOUS FEELING I'LL PUT ON RESERVE
FOR THAT SPECIAL ONE THAT'S TRULY DESERVING OF LOVE

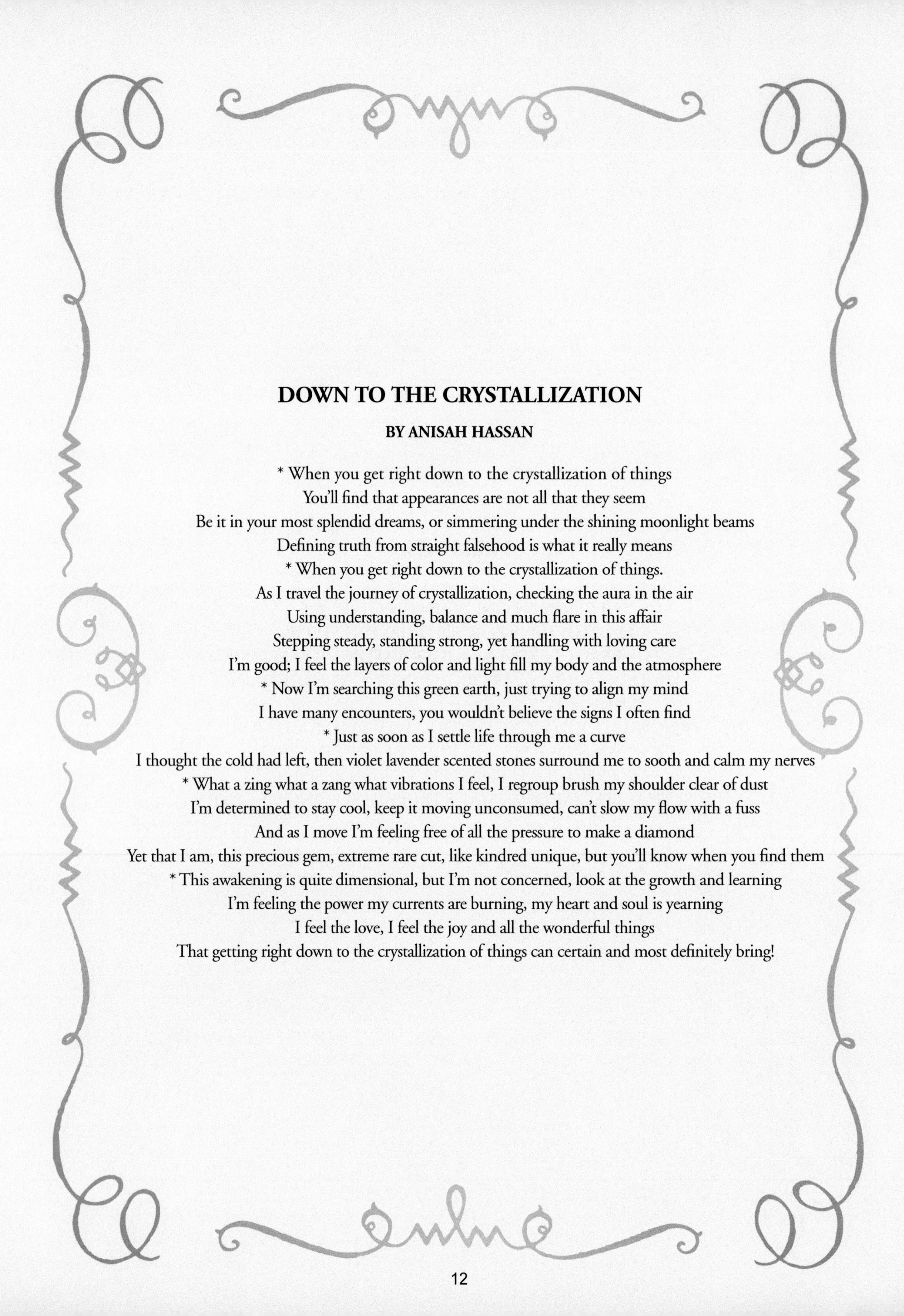

DOWN TO THE CRYSTALLIZATION

BY ANISAH HASSAN

* When you get right down to the crystallization of things
You'll find that appearances are not all that they seem
Be it in your most splendid dreams, or simmering under the shining moonlight beams
Defining truth from straight falsehood is what it really means
* When you get right down to the crystallization of things.
As I travel the journey of crystallization, checking the aura in the air
Using understanding, balance and much flare in this affair
Stepping steady, standing strong, yet handling with loving care
I'm good; I feel the layers of color and light fill my body and the atmosphere
* Now I'm searching this green earth, just trying to align my mind
I have many encounters, you wouldn't believe the signs I often find
* Just as soon as I settle life through me a curve
I thought the cold had left, then violet lavender scented stones surround me to sooth and calm my nerves
* What a zing what a zang what vibrations I feel, I regroup brush my shoulder clear of dust
I'm determined to stay cool, keep it moving unconsumed, can't slow my flow with a fuss
And as I move I'm feeling free of all the pressure to make a diamond
Yet that I am, this precious gem, extreme rare cut, like kindred unique, but you'll know when you find them
* This awakening is quite dimensional, but I'm not concerned, look at the growth and learning
I'm feeling the power my currents are burning, my heart and soul is yearning
I feel the love, I feel the joy and all the wonderful things
That getting right down to the crystallization of things can certain and most definitely bring!

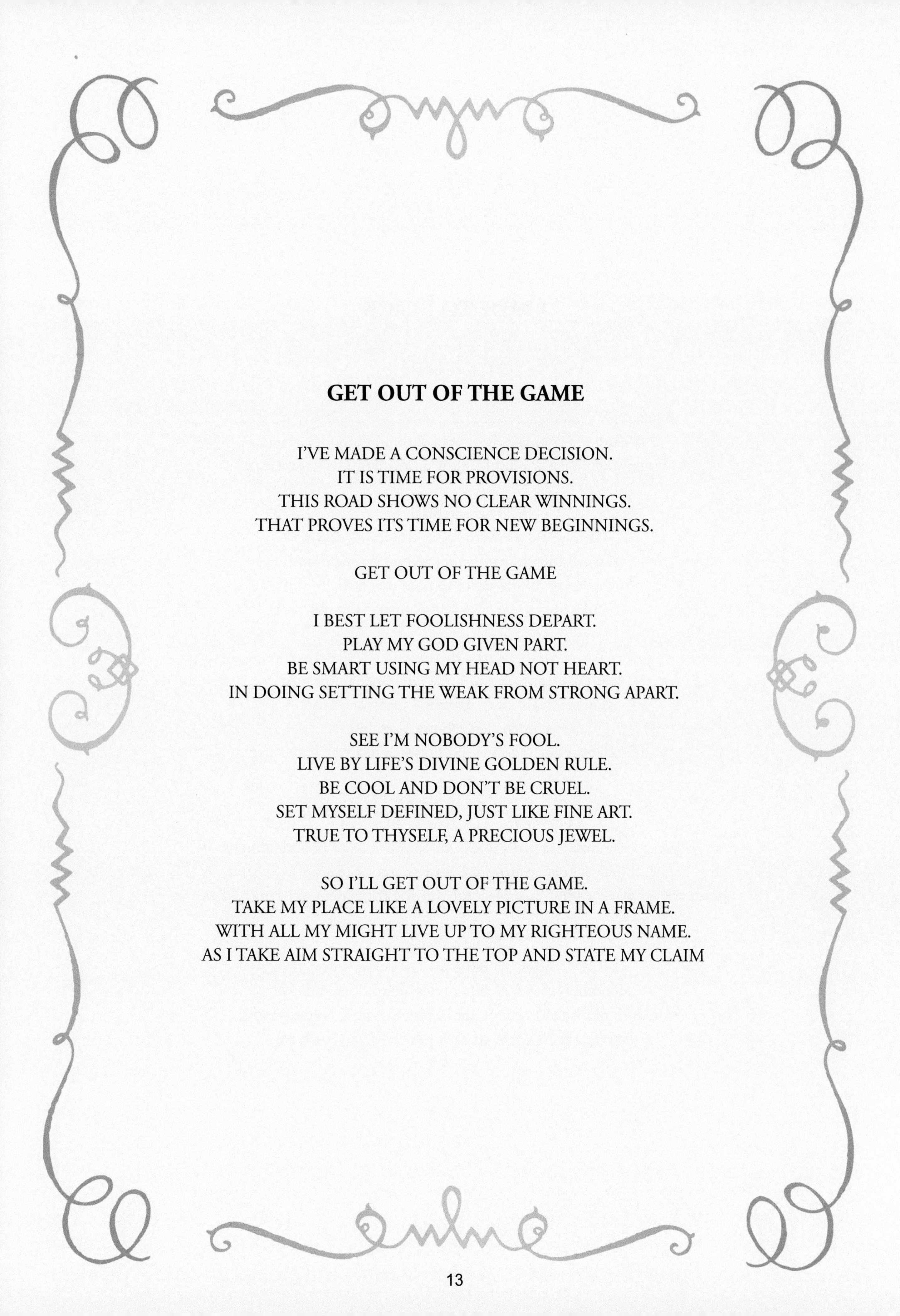

GET OUT OF THE GAME

I'VE MADE A CONSCIENCE DECISION.
IT IS TIME FOR PROVISIONS.
THIS ROAD SHOWS NO CLEAR WINNINGS.
THAT PROVES ITS TIME FOR NEW BEGINNINGS.

GET OUT OF THE GAME

I BEST LET FOOLISHNESS DEPART.
PLAY MY GOD GIVEN PART.
BE SMART USING MY HEAD NOT HEART.
IN DOING SETTING THE WEAK FROM STRONG APART.

SEE I'M NOBODY'S FOOL.
LIVE BY LIFE'S DIVINE GOLDEN RULE.
BE COOL AND DON'T BE CRUEL.
SET MYSELF DEFINED, JUST LIKE FINE ART.
TRUE TO THYSELF, A PRECIOUS JEWEL.

SO I'LL GET OUT OF THE GAME.
TAKE MY PLACE LIKE A LOVELY PICTURE IN A FRAME.
WITH ALL MY MIGHT LIVE UP TO MY RIGHTEOUS NAME.
AS I TAKE AIM STRAIGHT TO THE TOP AND STATE MY CLAIM

I FADE TO BLACK

I fade to black
When I hear things that are not fact.
When there's mad ignorance in the midst and I will give no slack.
When ones approach is so bold with no thought or tact.
When troubles all around I simply do my best not to overreact.

I fade to black
If my world seems to come crumbling down.
If so call friends get missing and cannot be found.
If the storms of life seems to pour down all around.
If I just can't seem to find common ground.

I fade to black
Can't just can't deal with the ignorance in the air.
Can just walk away, because I really don't care.
Can I settle for less, oh my God do I dare.
Can listen to more nonsense, NO I'll step just watch and stare.

I fade to black
I never knew I was to be your fool.
I never knew you had plans to use me as your box of tricks and tools.
I never knew you would stoop so low of me to use.
I never knew I was the topic of subject for you and companies mockery and amuse.

I fade to black
About to rattle my last nerve.
About hear dishes of defamation that I don't deserve.
About to think I'm to accept the deception you're about to serve.
About fade to black, sit back preserved and reserved.

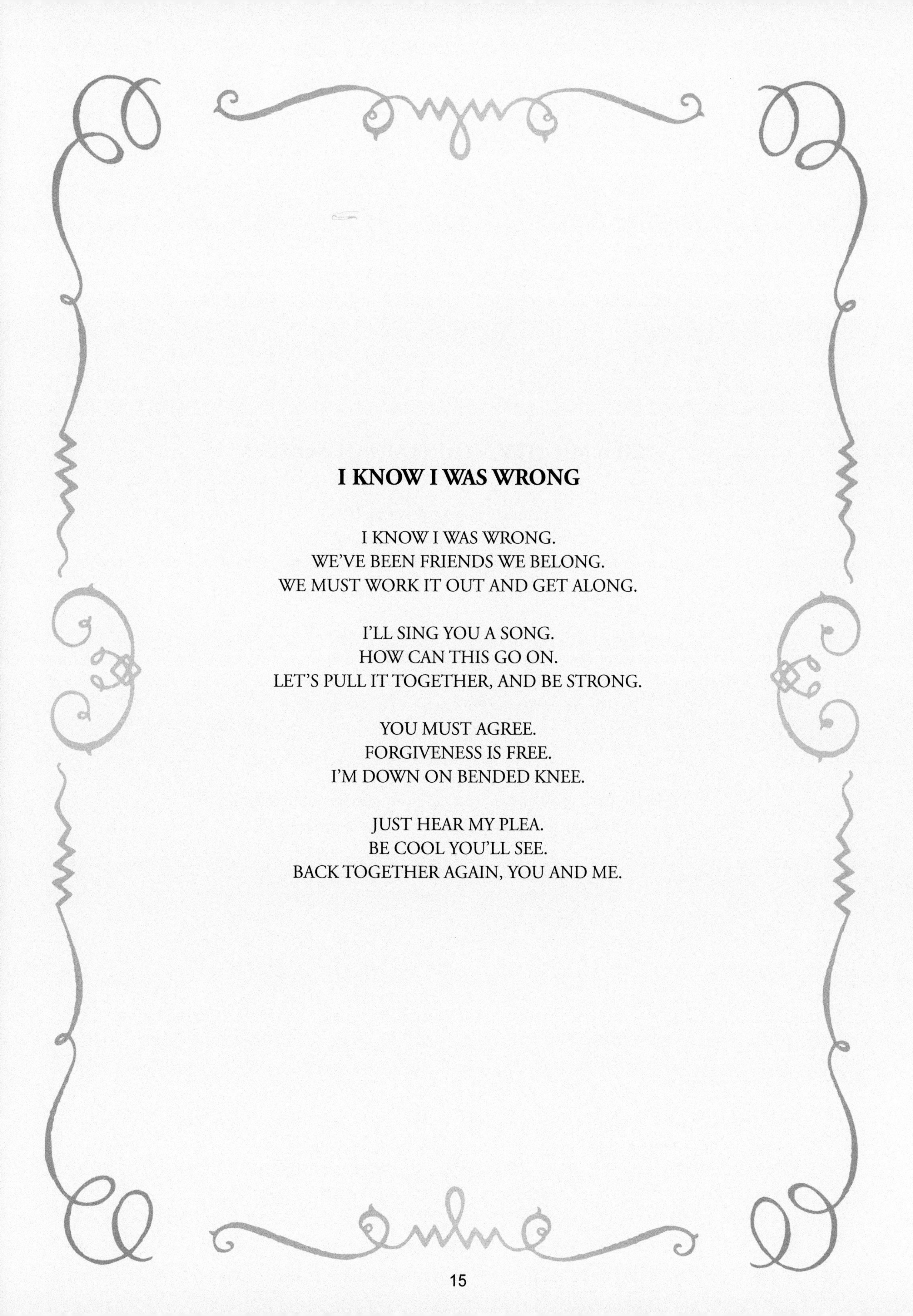

I KNOW I WAS WRONG

I KNOW I WAS WRONG.
WE'VE BEEN FRIENDS WE BELONG.
WE MUST WORK IT OUT AND GET ALONG.

I'LL SING YOU A SONG.
HOW CAN THIS GO ON.
LET'S PULL IT TOGETHER, AND BE STRONG.

YOU MUST AGREE.
FORGIVENESS IS FREE.
I'M DOWN ON BENDED KNEE.

JUST HEAR MY PLEA.
BE COOL YOU'LL SEE.
BACK TOGETHER AGAIN, YOU AND ME.

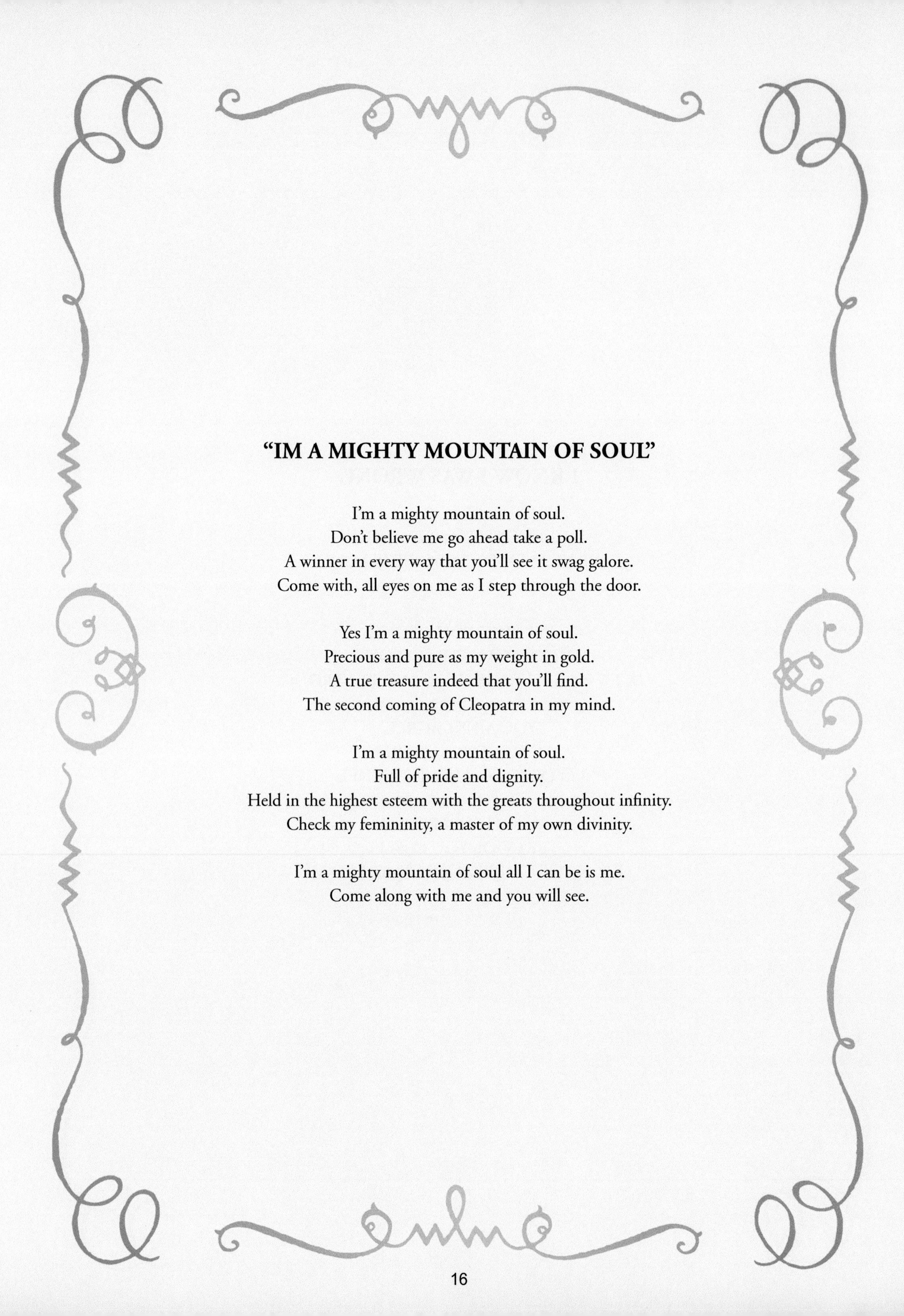

"IM A MIGHTY MOUNTAIN OF SOUL"

I'm a mighty mountain of soul.
Don't believe me go ahead take a poll.
A winner in every way that you'll see it swag galore.
Come with, all eyes on me as I step through the door.

Yes I'm a mighty mountain of soul.
Precious and pure as my weight in gold.
A true treasure indeed that you'll find.
The second coming of Cleopatra in my mind.

I'm a mighty mountain of soul.
Full of pride and dignity.
Held in the highest esteem with the greats throughout infinity.
Check my femininity, a master of my own divinity.

I'm a mighty mountain of soul all I can be is me.
Come along with me and you will see.

IS IT YES

IS IT IN THE WAY YOU WALK
IS IT IN THE WAY YOU TALK
IS IT THE SWEET WAY YOU SAY HELLO

IS IT IN THE WAY YOU FLOW
IS IT IN THAT SPECIAL GLOW
IS IT THAT SPARK IN YOUR EYE THAT I KNOW

I AM REMINISCENT OF
THE ATTENTION THAT YOU SHOWED
MY WAY AT FIRST SIGHT, CAN IT BE LOVE

Yes you're all that I dream of
Yes we fit like hand and glove
Yes it's that sweet thing that they call LOVE.

IT'S YOU THAT I ADORE

IT'S YOU DEAR ONE, THAT I ADORE.
I'M HERE, I'M WAITING, COME KNOCK ON MY DOOR.
THERE'S TREATS FOR YOU NO WAY TO IGNORE.
JUST WAIT TILL YOU SEE WHAT I HAVE IN STORE.

YOU ARE A TREASURE FROM YOUR HEAD TO THE FLOOR.
TOGETHER WE'LL MAKE MUSIC, WHO CAN ASK FOR MORE.
THERE'S SO MANY THINGS FOR US TO EXPLORE.
COME NEAR ME, GET CLOSE, WHAT ARE YOU WAITING FOR.

THAT'S BETTER, I FEEL YOU, COME CLOSER AND TAKE A TOUR.
WE'RE HERE TOGETHER BRINGING LOVE NOT WAR.
NO BORE, NO CHORE JUST PLEASURE GALORE.
YOU'RE BEAUTIFUL, INSIDE AND OUT, I'M READY TO EXPLORE
MY IT'S YOU I ADORE EVEN MORE AND MORE

"JUST GIVE THEM HELL"

Just give them hell when they come from the left
Just give them hell when unprepared and fail to prep
I'll tell you I'm no aggressor I'm one who's first all for peace.
But know you've been warned to desist and cease.

Why ignite a fire when barely equipped.
Why inflict self-harm to leave weary and whipped.
Peace I say Peace is the way to go.
Or stand to endure a a grievous blow.

All over and around is where I'll be.
Full blast, straight shot, all you'll see is me.
Don't get me wrong I'm kind you'll see.
Just don't mistake me for timid, meek, or weak.

So when one comes to be a disturbance
Just give them hell, so they'll never forget
They'll surely will deserving it!

KEEP IT COMING

I FEEL SO GOOD LIKE I NATURALLY SHOULD.
I FEEL SO NICE GOT TO SAY IT TWICE
I'M BEAUTIFUL LIKE BIRDS OF PARADISE.
MY SPIRITUAL GROWTH WELL THERE'S NO PRICE.
MOST HIGH KEEP MY BLESSINGS COMING.

WHY MUST I CRY IN THE DARKNESS OF NIGHT.
THE BOOK SAYS PRAYER'S PRESCRIBED AND ALSO FIGHT.
OH WELL THAT'S WHAT I'LL DO RIGHT DOWN TO THE END.
WITH THE MOST HIGH ON MY SIDE I KNOW I'LL WIN.

LIKE A BIRD IN THE SKY I'M SOARING HIGH.
SWIM THE STORMY SEA, STILL GOOD GOD FEEL OUT OF SIGHT.
I MUST SAY LIFE'S BEEN KIND TO ME
WELCOME TO MY WORLD AND YOU WILL SEE.

WALK IN MY SHOES SEE HOW BLESSED I BE.
AT THE TOP OF MY GAME ON EVERY DEGREE,
MAKING SURE TO DOT MY I'S AND CROSS MY T'S.
COME WITH, COME WITH AND ROLL WITH ME.

COME FORTH LAY BESIDE ME DRINK UP SOME SUN.
LET IT KISS YOUR FACE,OVER TAKE YOU TILL THE GOLDEN TIME OF DAY COME.
COME WITH ME, YOUR FRIEND OF GOOD COMPANY.
PLEASE KEEP MY BLESSING COMING MOST HIGH.
TOGETHER WE'LL CONQUER ALL I'M SURE YOU'LL AGREE.

I NEVER KNEW

I NEVER KNEW THAT YOU COULD BE SO CRUEL.
I NEVER KNEW THAT YOU WHERE AROUND THE WAY ACTING A FOOL.
I NEVER KNEW THAT YOU EXPECTED ME TO BE YOUR STEPPING STOOL.
I NEVER KNEW YOU'D LEAVE ME CRYING ON MY KNEES WITH TEARS, A POOL.

NOW I KNOW AND OWE YOU CAUSE I'M STRONGER NOW.
NOW I KNOW, THE CURTAINS CLOSING SO TAKE YOUR BOW.
NOW I KNOW LIFE CAN BE BEAUTIFUL, I MUST SAY WOW.
NOW THAT I KNOW AND SAY NEVER AGAIN TO YOU.
SO GO CENTER STAGE AND TRY WORKING THE CROWD.

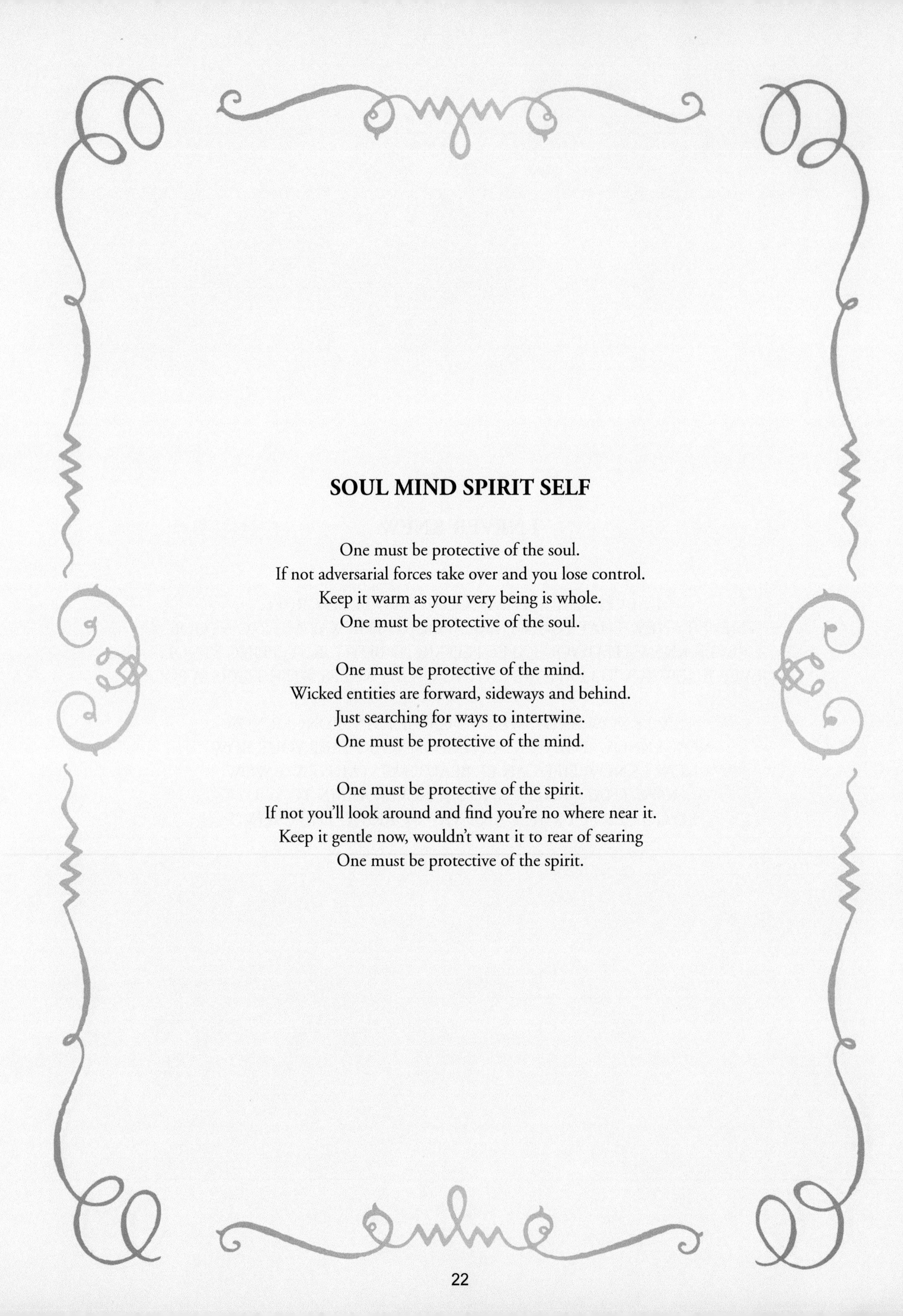

SOUL MIND SPIRIT SELF

One must be protective of the soul.
If not adversarial forces take over and you lose control.
Keep it warm as your very being is whole.
One must be protective of the soul.

One must be protective of the mind.
Wicked entities are forward, sideways and behind.
Just searching for ways to intertwine.
One must be protective of the mind.

One must be protective of the spirit.
If not you'll look around and find you're no where near it.
Keep it gentle now, wouldn't want it to rear of searing
One must be protective of the spirit.

LET MY RECORD SHOW

MY LOVE IS REAL FOR YOU, SO LET MY RECORD SHOW.
FROM THE BOTTOM TO THE TOP, GOT TO LET YOU KNOW.
MY STYLE SLOW AND EASY, I JUST LET IT FLOW.
AND IT'S FOR YOU, YOUR FACE IS ALL AGLOW.
I'VE STATED MY CASE AND FELT YOU HAD TO KNOW.
MY TESTIMONIES OUT, I'VE LET MY FEELING GO.

LET MY RECORD SHOW YOU'RE ON MY MIND.
LET MY RECORD SHOW MY TYPE OF TREASURES ARE HARD TO FIND.
LET MY RECORD SHOW TOGETHER WE'RE REFINED AND SHINE.
LET MY RECORD SHOW INTERTWINED WE'LL TAKE FLIGHT AND FLY, LEAVING THE WORLD BEHIND.

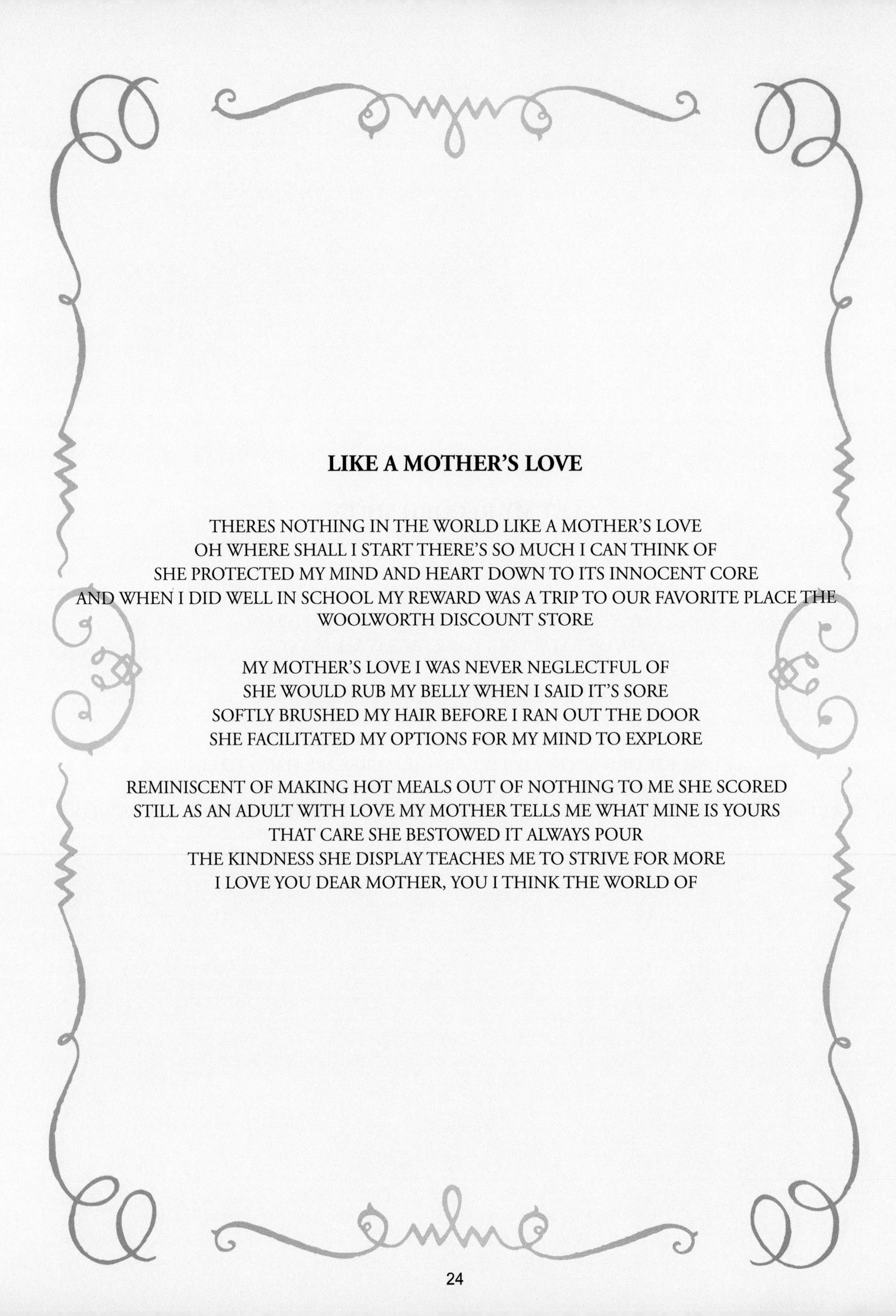

LIKE A MOTHER'S LOVE

THERES NOTHING IN THE WORLD LIKE A MOTHER'S LOVE
OH WHERE SHALL I START THERE'S SO MUCH I CAN THINK OF
SHE PROTECTED MY MIND AND HEART DOWN TO ITS INNOCENT CORE
AND WHEN I DID WELL IN SCHOOL MY REWARD WAS A TRIP TO OUR FAVORITE PLACE THE WOOLWORTH DISCOUNT STORE

MY MOTHER'S LOVE I WAS NEVER NEGLECTFUL OF
SHE WOULD RUB MY BELLY WHEN I SAID IT'S SORE
SOFTLY BRUSHED MY HAIR BEFORE I RAN OUT THE DOOR
SHE FACILITATED MY OPTIONS FOR MY MIND TO EXPLORE

REMINISCENT OF MAKING HOT MEALS OUT OF NOTHING TO ME SHE SCORED
STILL AS AN ADULT WITH LOVE MY MOTHER TELLS ME WHAT MINE IS YOURS
THAT CARE SHE BESTOWED IT ALWAYS POUR
THE KINDNESS SHE DISPLAY TEACHES ME TO STRIVE FOR MORE
I LOVE YOU DEAR MOTHER, YOU I THINK THE WORLD OF

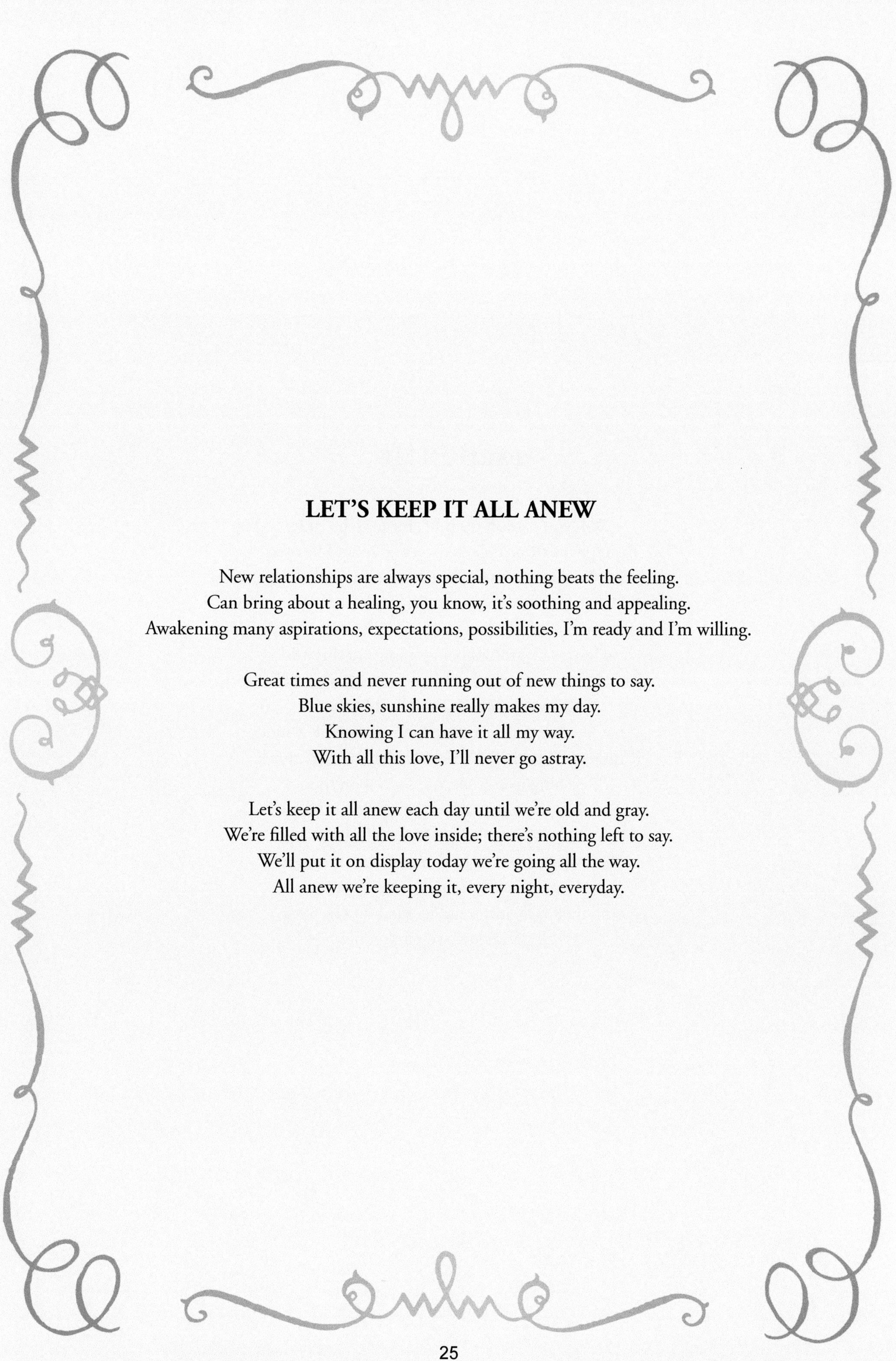

LET'S KEEP IT ALL ANEW

New relationships are always special, nothing beats the feeling.
Can bring about a healing, you know, it's soothing and appealing.
Awakening many aspirations, expectations, possibilities, I'm ready and I'm willing.

Great times and never running out of new things to say.
Blue skies, sunshine really makes my day.
Knowing I can have it all my way.
With all this love, I'll never go astray.

Let's keep it all anew each day until we're old and gray.
We're filled with all the love inside; there's nothing left to say.
We'll put it on display today we're going all the way.
All anew we're keeping it, every night, everyday.

PARDON ME

Will you pardon me don't mean to be rude
I simply just won't allow myself to sit and be used
Won't be that one to be tossed up as anyone's amuse
Refuse to be viewed as one's complete and utter ignorant fool
Please pardon me for I'm that one that follows life's golden rule
Don't walk around being smug and shrewd
Say what you want or must, it's me and it's what I choose
To love, to like and sooth all bruised
What joy those one gets throwing salt on the wound
Pardon me if bothered with troubles I'm there quick
Reaching to console you soon soon soon
So when life is through those inevitable blows
No worries relax you'll rise all aglow.
See where there's light you blossom and grow
No woes, no sighs, no sorrows just be.
And if all fails, just stand let God do His work.
I'll stand down so pardon me

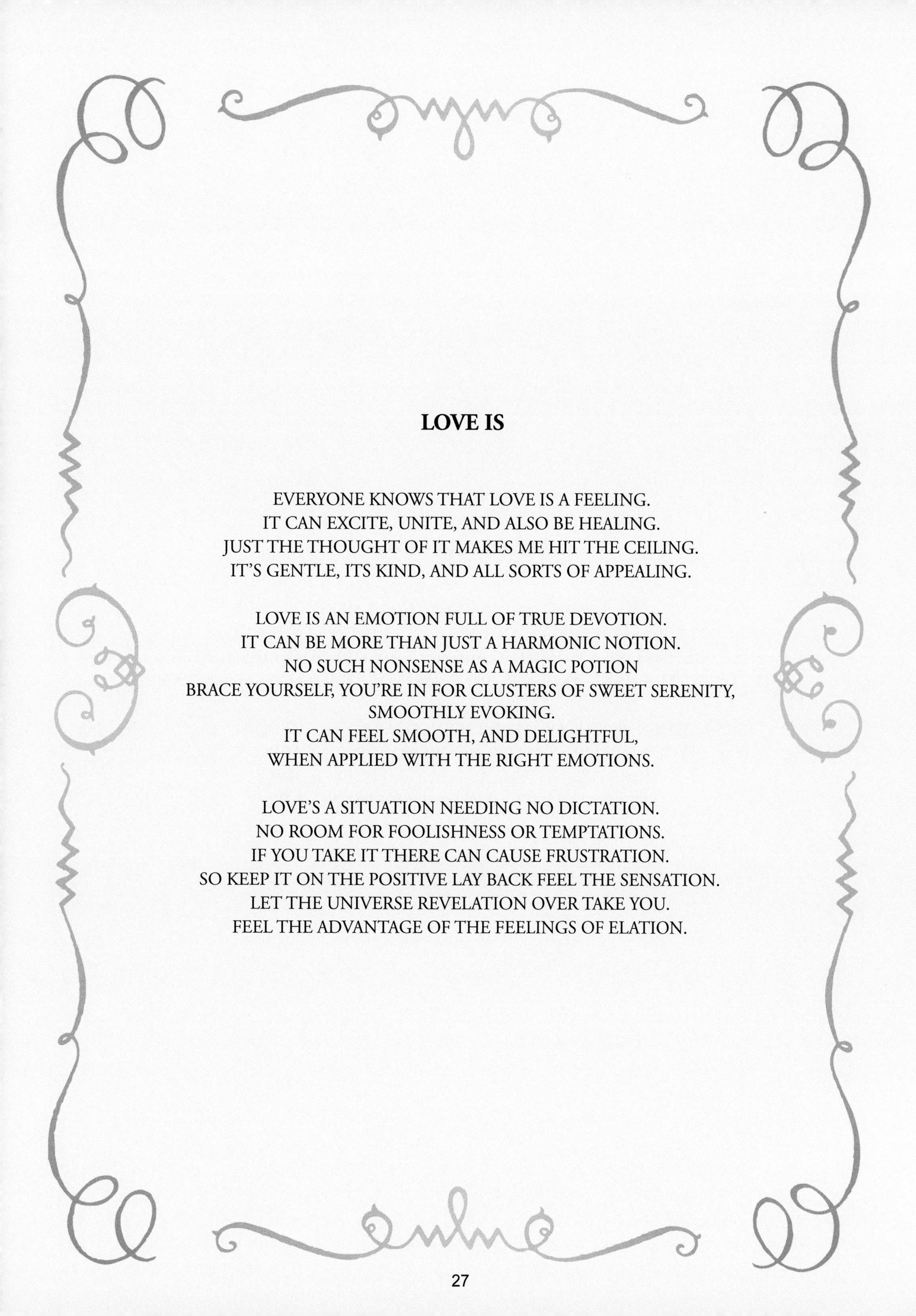

LOVE IS

EVERYONE KNOWS THAT LOVE IS A FEELING.
IT CAN EXCITE, UNITE, AND ALSO BE HEALING.
JUST THE THOUGHT OF IT MAKES ME HIT THE CEILING.
IT'S GENTLE, ITS KIND, AND ALL SORTS OF APPEALING.

LOVE IS AN EMOTION FULL OF TRUE DEVOTION.
IT CAN BE MORE THAN JUST A HARMONIC NOTION.
NO SUCH NONSENSE AS A MAGIC POTION
BRACE YOURSELF, YOU'RE IN FOR CLUSTERS OF SWEET SERENITY,
SMOOTHLY EVOKING.
IT CAN FEEL SMOOTH, AND DELIGHTFUL,
WHEN APPLIED WITH THE RIGHT EMOTIONS.

LOVE'S A SITUATION NEEDING NO DICTATION.
NO ROOM FOR FOOLISHNESS OR TEMPTATIONS.
IF YOU TAKE IT THERE CAN CAUSE FRUSTRATION.
SO KEEP IT ON THE POSITIVE LAY BACK FEEL THE SENSATION.
LET THE UNIVERSE REVELATION OVER TAKE YOU.
FEEL THE ADVANTAGE OF THE FEELINGS OF ELATION.

MY HEART SING

IF YOU CAN HEAR MY HEART SING.
YOU'LL SAY I SIMPLY CAN'T BELIEVE THIS TYPE OF THING .
IT SOUNDS LIKE A HUMMING BIRD ON THE FIRST DAY OF SPRING.
MAKES THE TULIPS HANG AROUND, BUNCHED TOGETHER TO SWAY AND SWING.

WHEN YOU HEAR THE MELODY THAT MY HEART SING.
YOU'RE REMINDED OF THE DREAMY VIOLIN STRINGS.
MORE DELIGHTFUL AS THE TEMPLE BELL DING
SHINING BEAUTIFULLY LIKE A WEDDING RING

"NOT TO WORRY"

Not to worry my dear for I am always near.
For when you're feeling sad I'll appear.
To sing sweet songs to you.
There's simply nothing I won't do.
I'll build the highest mountain for your view.

I'll hold your hand for a while.
Just to make you smile.
Instilling peace and blessing by the miles.
That's nothing for me, I'll swim the widest sea, it's only me being me.
Not to worry you'll see, my promise to you, beauty on every degree.

Not to worry, I'll always protect you.
I'll come from near or far, no distance impossible, no place to far
Even if it means traveling the highest star.

Not to worry when you feel alone.
I'll zoom you to a glorious zone, where elements of happiness is grown.
Very easy for you to find, follow the signs of your mind, be surprised at what you find
Though the galaxies of time, I've stored good vibes to keep you strong.

No fears no tear, I'll back you though the years on that you can depend.
My love is true, my friendship too, for you there is no end.
Not to worry it's not a loan, it's yours and yours to own.
No one can take it away.

This is for you my eternal rhyme.
Right with the "Sublime", that never sleeps with time.

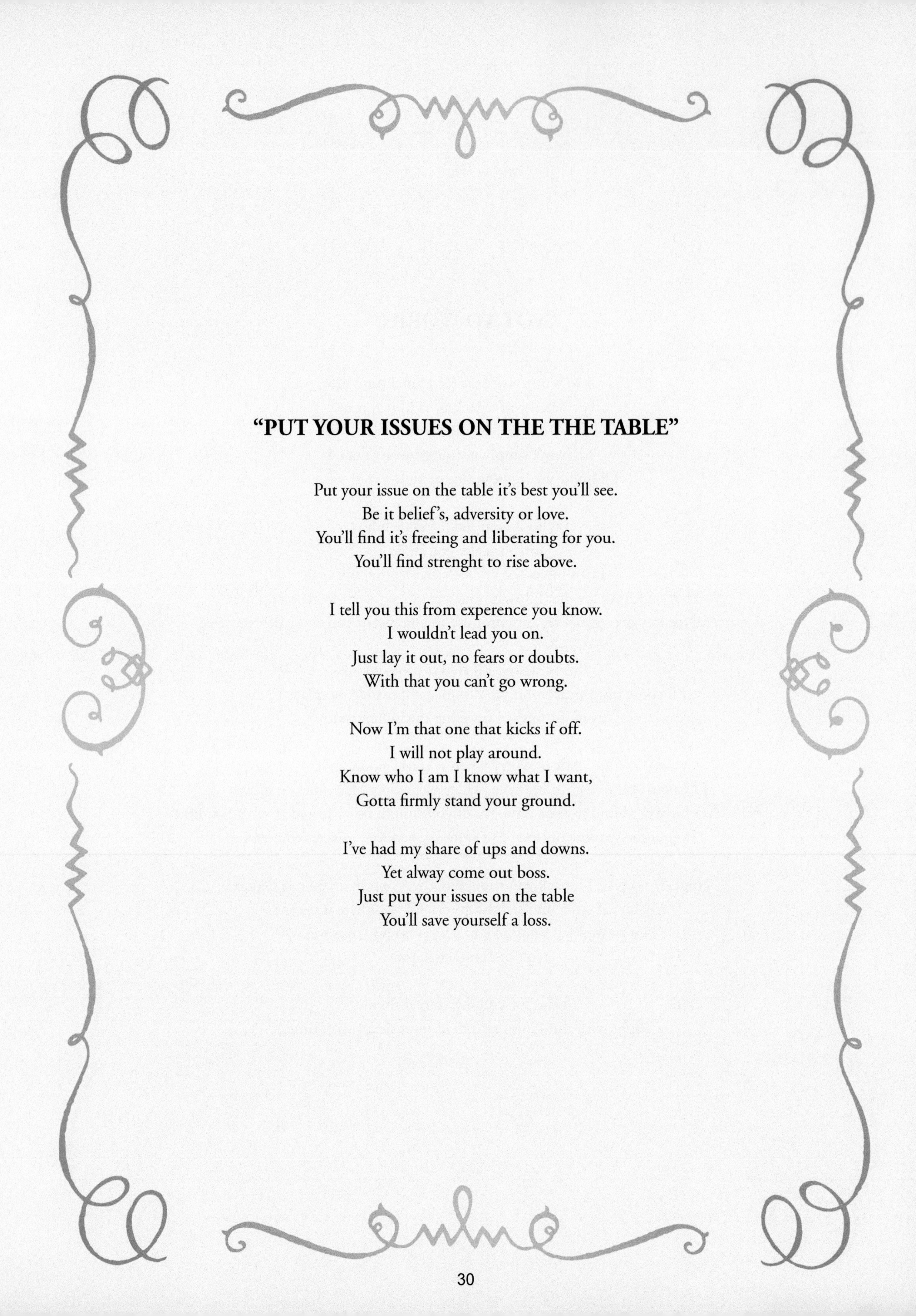

"PUT YOUR ISSUES ON THE THE TABLE"

Put your issue on the table it's best you'll see.
Be it belief's, adversity or love.
You'll find it's freeing and liberating for you.
You'll find strenght to rise above.

I tell you this from experence you know.
I wouldn't lead you on.
Just lay it out, no fears or doubts.
With that you can't go wrong.

Now I'm that one that kicks if off.
I will not play around.
Know who I am I know what I want,
Gotta firmly stand your ground.

I've had my share of ups and downs.
Yet alway come out boss.
Just put your issues on the table
You'll save yourself a loss.

WHAT IS YOUR PLATFORM

WHAT IS YOUR PLATFORM ALL ABOUT?
DO YOU SIMPLY JUST TO STAND THERE TO HEAR YOURSELF TALK?
ARE YOU SPEAKING FOR ENRICHMENT FOR ALL WHEN YOU OPEN YOUR MOUTH?
THEN GO I'M WITH YOU AND I LOVE TO BE TAUGHT.

REMEMBER WHERE THERE'S MASSES LARGE SCALES HUGE PLATFORMS.
NOT TO BE MINCED AND TIED IN WITH THE NORM.
AND WITH THE WISH TO BE HEARD AND MAKE A DIFFERENCE TO THE MASSES.
NOT SIMPLY MAKE STATEMENTS WITH NO MERIT THERE'S NO PASSES.

I'M JUST THAT ONE YOU'VE BEEN WAITING FOR.
NOT COMING WITH STATEMENTS OF BARE NECESSITIES, BUT SO MUCH MORE.
LET'S LOOK AT ALL THE WOE'S OF THE WORLD.
LET'S BREAK ALL CHAINS THAT BIND US AND KICK OPEN DOORS.

HOPE YOUR RECORDS SHOW YOUR WORKS AND ALL THAT MATTERS.
HOPE YOU'RE A MAGNETIC FIGURE WITH VALUES SO POWERFUL THAT BAD THINGS SHATTERS.
NEVER MIND ALL NAYSAYERS AND HATERS LET THEM DO WHAT THEY DO.
AS YOU SHINE AND SHIMMER AS YOUR BRILLIANCE SHINE THROUGH.

And WHEN THE JOBS DONE THANK THE MOST COMPASSIONATE FOR WHAT YOU SOUGHT.
FOR WHAT YOU TRULY STEP FORTH WITH WHAT YOUR PLATFORMS ABOUT?

EVERYTIME I TURN AROUND

Everytime I turn around I'm having thoughts of you..
I try to think of something else can't shake you from my view
All that I know is that I'm though can't calm my feeling they're true.
It took a while to try to think just didn't have a clue.

Now everytime I turn around I smell your nice cologne.
It makes me think and wonder what if we were alone.
Thoughts flow, whirling unbeknown I'm in a whirl.
It sends me in a zone.

Oh everytime I turn around it's you that's all I see.
I try to to drink my herbal tea, but with you is where I'd rather be.
I could go ski, shake my neighbhors peach tree or sail the deep blue sea.
Oh what the heck I'm stuck on you and in love that's clear to me.

It's every time I turn around I'm feeling kind of blue.
My friends all tell me come on girl, he'll call you when he's through.
I guess they're right despite my right to sit and dream of you.
But whew what a man, can't understand keep having deja vu.

KISSED BY DEJA VU

One time in my going, sunset was coming into fold.
Warm breeze starts flowing, wrapping itself around my soul.
The scenes mystic is showing, feel free my hair caressing my face.
I welcome it's embrace.
The beauty brought a strangeness, I stood to take a moments look.
Just so ahh inspring, an experience not found in a book.
The feeling bring forth knowing, as I realize whats happening.
I've been kissed by deja vu

Next the vivid huge clouds, oh yes I see them by the miles.
Fragrance fill the surroundings, envoking raised brows and smile.
The sky has changed right into, a view I know, yet known by few coming in though and true.
I'd like to say it's voliet, yet I know that's not the hue.
Then come to say its lilac with hints of gold and indigo blue.
Yet smile and know it's for me, I've seen before it's plan to see.
The sight brings forth the knowing, that this is certainly not new to me.
I've been kissed by deja vu.

This inconcievable creation, saying be cool you are okay.
Filled with such elation, saying fall back give your spirt it's way.
No need for explanation, vibrations stir and say it your day relive this familiar display.
Last, here I am soaring, I know I've been here before.
Going through the motions flowing unbrided no control.
I seize this time that's showing, with closed eyes the cold fades old.
And the warmth takes hold my soul.

Again comes forth my knowing, I lend my cheek allowing it to happen again.
I'M BEING KISSED BY DEJA VU.

ALL THAT I AM

Take these hands and don't let go
I'll hold you near enabling fearlessness to grow
Take my hands, use them any day
When you need a strong grip, hold tight,
I'm not tired, no how, no way
No need for explanation, I'm always here
Here's my shoulder, lean on it, I'm near my dear
These ears, these ears are non judgmental
Main purpose to listen, I care, I'm gentle
My heart it's yours, with love galore
When your spirits low and you can take no more
And these eyes will watch like a hawk
They'll observe at close range, protecting when adversarial forces lark
Here are my feet to support the weight
When the trials of life present themselves: steady, steady little margin for mistakes
You have my arms, to carry your load
When it's dark and lonely,
I know the world seems so cold
My voice is here to state your case
Advocating just for you,
watch out I'm bringing the BASS
These two strong legs will run to you
Be it triumphs, depth of pain (stress not) I'm your one woman crew
When your soul gets weary, and you can't sleep
I'll ask The Protector from all Harm
to grant you peace
Remember, here I am, for I love you, it's endless,
no cut off time
Call whenever, my loves evergreen with strength of ivy leaves, all things possible when bathe
by The Sublime!

CAN WE FIND WHATS MISSING

I feel the warmth that enfolds, while laying around dreaming with my head in the clouds but i don't feel you..

Can we find whats missing?

I see a beautiful purple sky with streaks of pink and indigo,
but i don't see you.

Can we find whats missing?

I hear the sound of miles trumpet playing the sweetest melody just for me, but i don't hear you.

Can we find whats missing?.

I smell the soothing scent of mint and anise, as i sip my tea, but i don't smell you.

Can we find whats missing?

I taste the delicious flavor of a cherry so sweet, but i can't taste you.

Can we find whats missing.

All these little lovely things that makes life a treat, hmmmmm, all the best too us all, is what i'm wishing.

LIFE

DANCING IN THE RAIN IS FREEING TO ME.
SAILING UNDER THE SUN IS ALL THAT IT COULD BE
WALKING UNDER THE MOONLIGHT WITH MY HONEY DELIGHTS ME YOU SEE.
LYING UNDER THE STARS, MAKE'S ME FEEL SO CARE FREE.

YES FLOATING ON THE OCEAN GIVES ME SUCH A THRILL.
CLIMBING THE HIGHEST MOUNTAIN SEEMS SO UNREAL.
SPRINTING CROSS COUNTRY SENDS LAUGHTER THOUGH MY BONES.
HOPES AND DREAMS THOUGH MY MINDS SEED OF LIGHT.
HELPS A SISTER/BROTHER CARRY ON.

IF I WERE

If I were a lunar moon I'd watch you as you sleep.
I'll hang around when you are down you'll never know a frown.

If I were a celestial star I'd gleem on you all night.
I'd ride your arm just like a charm and keep you safe from harm.

If I were the dazzingly sun I shine on you all day.
I'd make you glad, you'll know no sad and lighten paths you'll style in everyway.

If I were a ,gentle sea, I'd catch you when you fall.
I'd bounce you back when you're adrift and be your all in all.

Now if I were a pretty tune, I'll harmonize your songs.
We'll rock the world with much swag, just as strong.
Together we can't go wrong!

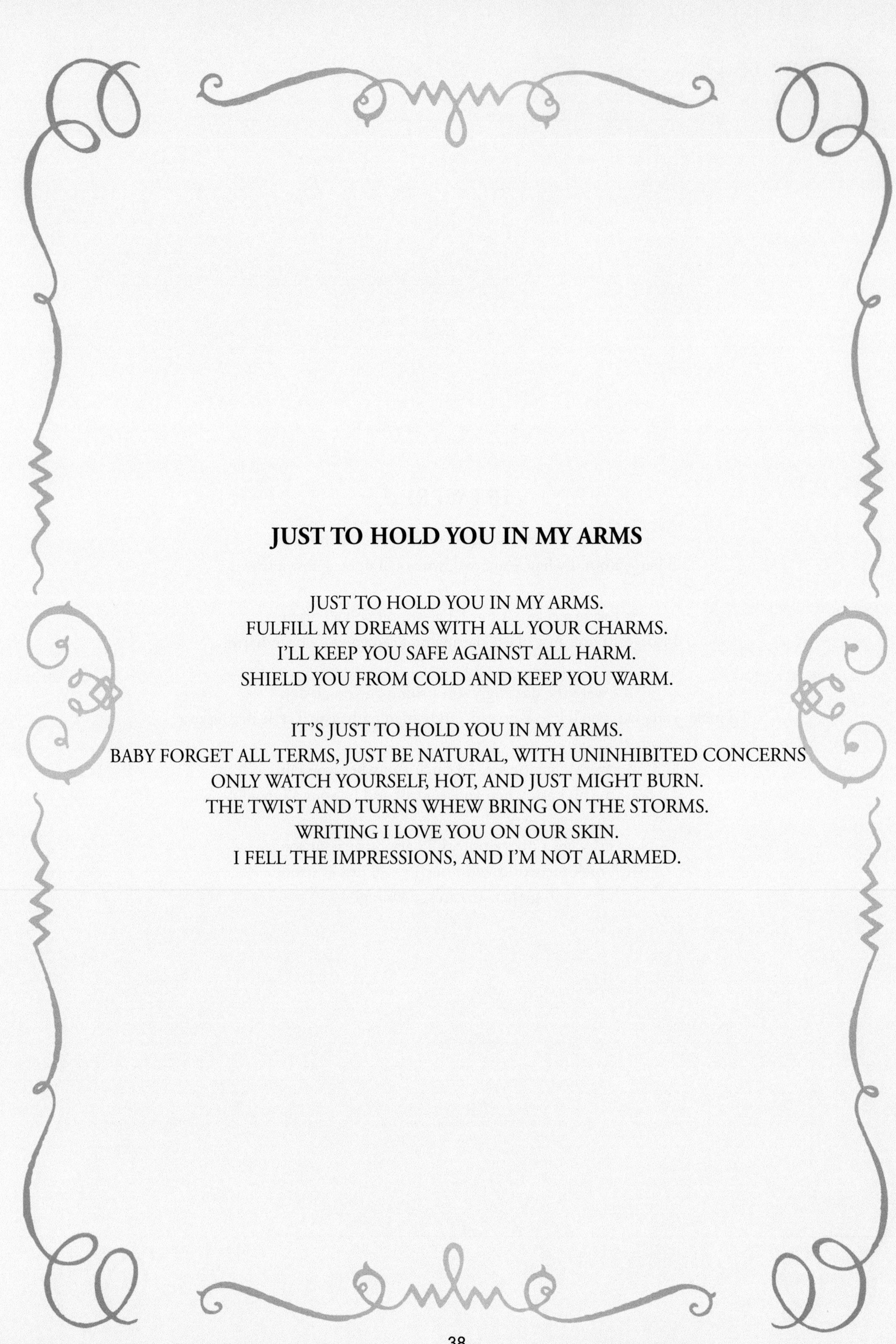

JUST TO HOLD YOU IN MY ARMS

JUST TO HOLD YOU IN MY ARMS.
FULFILL MY DREAMS WITH ALL YOUR CHARMS.
I'LL KEEP YOU SAFE AGAINST ALL HARM.
SHIELD YOU FROM COLD AND KEEP YOU WARM.

IT'S JUST TO HOLD YOU IN MY ARMS.
BABY FORGET ALL TERMS, JUST BE NATURAL, WITH UNINHIBITED CONCERNS
ONLY WATCH YOURSELF, HOT, AND JUST MIGHT BURN.
THE TWIST AND TURNS WHEW BRING ON THE STORMS.
WRITING I LOVE YOU ON OUR SKIN.
I FELL THE IMPRESSIONS, AND I'M NOT ALARMED.

MY LOVE

My love is warm like the sun that heats the earth.

My love is bright shining light throughout the universe.

My love is smooth covers the circumference of life's atmosphere.

My love is real, air tight seal, and I'm delighted to be here.

My love is true as sky's are blue, that I thought you knew.

My love just nurtures like all the essential things that's ever so good for you

So when you're high, low or somewhere in between.

Come for my love, it's good and plenty, enough for every being.

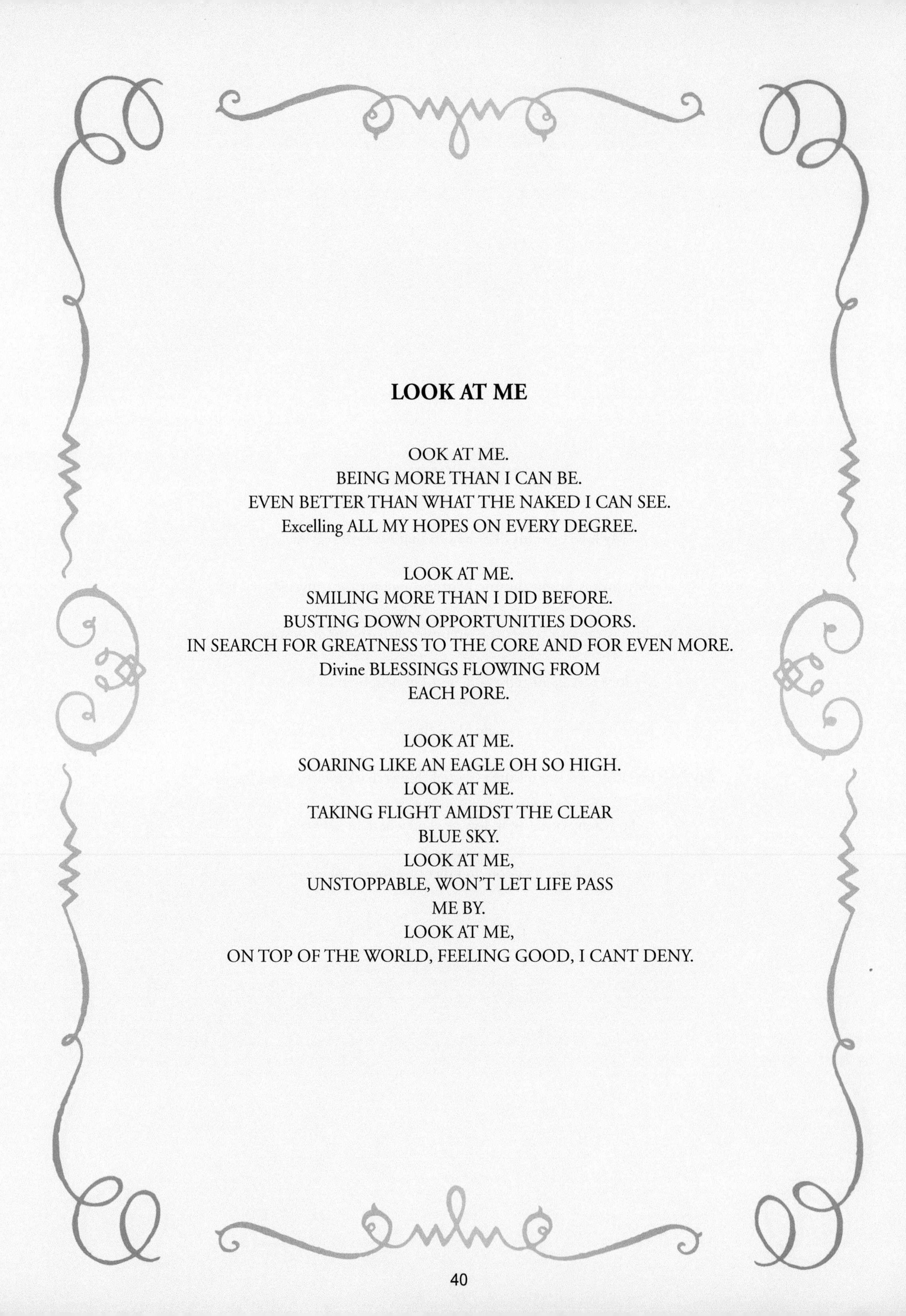

LOOK AT ME

OOK AT ME.
BEING MORE THAN I CAN BE.
EVEN BETTER THAN WHAT THE NAKED I CAN SEE.
Excelling ALL MY HOPES ON EVERY DEGREE.

LOOK AT ME.
SMILING MORE THAN I DID BEFORE.
BUSTING DOWN OPPORTUNITIES DOORS.
IN SEARCH FOR GREATNESS TO THE CORE AND FOR EVEN MORE.
Divine BLESSINGS FLOWING FROM
EACH PORE.

LOOK AT ME.
SOARING LIKE AN EAGLE OH SO HIGH.
LOOK AT ME.
TAKING FLIGHT AMIDST THE CLEAR
BLUE SKY.
LOOK AT ME,
UNSTOPPABLE, WON'T LET LIFE PASS
ME BY.
LOOK AT ME,
ON TOP OF THE WORLD, FEELING GOOD, I CANT DENY.

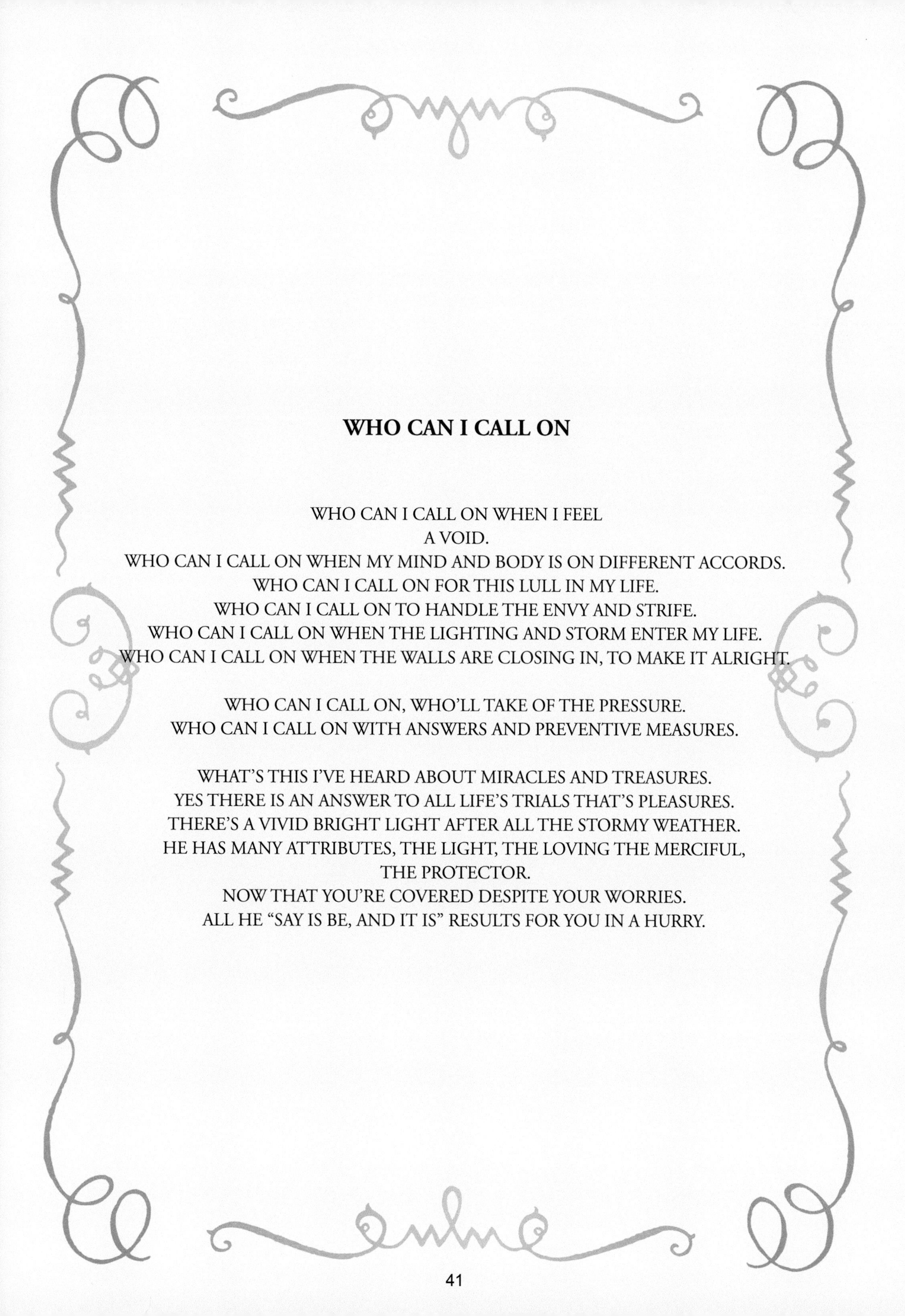

WHO CAN I CALL ON

WHO CAN I CALL ON WHEN I FEEL
A VOID.
WHO CAN I CALL ON WHEN MY MIND AND BODY IS ON DIFFERENT ACCORDS.
WHO CAN I CALL ON FOR THIS LULL IN MY LIFE.
WHO CAN I CALL ON TO HANDLE THE ENVY AND STRIFE.
WHO CAN I CALL ON WHEN THE LIGHTING AND STORM ENTER MY LIFE.
WHO CAN I CALL ON WHEN THE WALLS ARE CLOSING IN, TO MAKE IT ALRIGHT.

WHO CAN I CALL ON, WHO'LL TAKE OF THE PRESSURE.
WHO CAN I CALL ON WITH ANSWERS AND PREVENTIVE MEASURES.

WHAT'S THIS I'VE HEARD ABOUT MIRACLES AND TREASURES.
YES THERE IS AN ANSWER TO ALL LIFE'S TRIALS THAT'S PLEASURES.
THERE'S A VIVID BRIGHT LIGHT AFTER ALL THE STORMY WEATHER.
HE HAS MANY ATTRIBUTES, THE LIGHT, THE LOVING THE MERCIFUL,
THE PROTECTOR.
NOW THAT YOU'RE COVERED DESPITE YOUR WORRIES.
ALL HE "SAY IS BE, AND IT IS" RESULTS FOR YOU IN A HURRY.

Printed in the United States
by Baker & Taylor Publisher Services